Influence

by *Janet Munsil*

Influence
by Janet Munsil
is published by Missing Page Company
1245 Hewlett Place
Victoria BC V8S 4P6 Canada

Printed and Bound in Canada

Canadian Cataloguing Publication Data

Munsil, Janet
Influence
A play.

ISBN 978-0-9917342-1-4

Enquiries regarding production rights must be directed to:
jmunsil@shaw.ca
phone (250)884-6633

Influence was commissioned by Touchstone
Theatre and premiered at Performance Works
in Vancouver in 2008.

Original Cast

Hephaestus Donald Adams
John Keats Daniel Arnold
Benjamin Robert Haydon Mike Stack
Athena Colleen Wheeler
Apollo Frank Zotter

Creative Team

Director Katrina Dunn
Dramaturg Rachel Ditor
Assistant Director/Fight Choreographer
Joshua Reynolds
Set Design David Roberts
Lighting Design Jonathan Ryder
Costume Design Sheila White
Original Music and Sound Design Owen Belton
Stage Manager Marcella Hyde
Assistant Stage Manager Marijka Brusse
Production Manager Jeremy Baxter
Sculptor Heidi Wilkinson

The playwright would like to thank
the BC Arts Council, Banff Playwrights Colony,
and all of the workshop actors for their contributions
to the development of the play.

Characters

The Mortals

Benjamin Robert Haydon
History Painter (1786-1846)
John Keats
Medical student / poet (1795-1821)

The Immortals

Athena, Goddess of Wisdom and War
Apollo, God of Art and Medicine
Hephaestus, God of the Forge

Setting
Most of the action takes place in The Elgin Room of the British Museum, London, March 1, 1817. A large public room with benches, featuring the weathered pediment statuary and friezes of the Parthenon, from the collection of Lord Elgin.

Program Notes
Included at the end of this script are historical notes which appeared in the program for the Touchstone Theatre production.

John Keats by Benjamin Robert Haydon. Pen and Ink, 1816. NPG 3251
Reproduced with permission, National Portrait Gallery

Table of Contents

Act One

A dimly lit surgery, early 19th century. A man lies strapped to a table, restless and mumbling. A young doctor, Keats, is about to make an incision into his temple with a lancet. The room is lit by a single bright shaft of light from a skylight. He mumbles as Keats positions his head to one side and cuts into his temple.

A brief, blinding light, then darkness.

Lights up on the Elgin Room of the British Museum, March 1, 1817.

Haydon: How I envy you. I wish I could see them again for the first time. I thank God that when I first saw them, I was prepared to understand them. So. What do you think?

Keats: Sorry?

Haydon: Of the marbles?

Keats: Marbles.

Haydon: Lord Elgin's marbles! My gift to you, my legacy to the nation!

Keats: What do I think of the Elgin marbles?

Haydon: Yes, yes!

Keats: Uh . . . .

Haydon: Speak your mind.

Keats: Well, for one thing, they're very . . .

Haydon: Go on . . .

Keats: What I mean to say is—

Haydon: Yes?

Keats: What can one say?

Haydon: What is one saying?

Keats: I'm sorry, Haydon.

Haydon: I thought that of all the men of my circle, you might be intellectually, emotionally and spiritually prepared for these wonders. Was I mistaken? Was I over-eager to share them with you?

Keats: Please forgive me.

Haydon: 'Please forgive me Haydon, I'm so sorry Haydon.' Listen to yourself. Men of genius never apologize! Do you think that Phideas apologized for creating this perfect union of art and idea? What beauty! What grace! And this horse's head— what can be said but this? It is all truth. Truth and beauty, beauty and truth. In a nutshell.

Keats makes a note.

Keats: Beauty and Truth.

Haydon: Even nature bows to the great artist. A man of genius will make nature bend to him, kneel before him. He will force her into his service. Do you take my meaning?

Keats: Uh . . . I think so.

Haydon: And he will not release her until the thing is done! Then she may skip along and fashion her daisy chains. Eh?

Keats: This is a new language for me, antiquities, fragments.

Haydon: Of course! I'll translate to a language you understand. We will hone the scalpel of our intellect on these stones, eh? Then we shall begin our dissection, peel back the skin and flesh and peer into the centre of the mystery.

> *Haydon puts a second pair of spectacles on over a first pair to examine a detail on a sculpture. He runs his hand over the marble.*

Haydon: See the tension in the skin, as if bones and sinew were visible beneath. Touch it! Here the sculptor Phideas himself brought down his chisel and breathed life into stone! O, Immortal Phideas, creator of these noble works! What fire — what Genius! I bow and am grateful.

> *Haydon throws his arm around a statue.*

Haydon: These stones have been divine friends to whom I could turn in my darkest hour. To them I owe every principle of art I possess. To think that they once graced the Parthenon of Athens, a temple containing a gold and ivory statue of the Goddess Athena forty feet high! Ah, the ancients understood that only a monumental scale could suit an immortal subject.

Keats: Is that why your paintings are so large?

Haydon: Precisely! And how this annoys the fashionable patrons of today. "Your paintings are too large, our houses are too small, we have no room!" No room? I say: no taste! The greatest country in the world has no room for its most sublime mani-festation—History Painting? The expression of the greatest and most noble historic acts on a grand scale? And yet they'd happily commission some 'furniture painter' to render a portrait of great-granny nine feet high! Genius must express itself on a scale befitting its vision. And if genius must toil in poverty four years without a penny's pay over a single great work—what of it!

Keats: How is your great work coming along?

Haydon: The time for painting the divine head of Christ is at hand. I have had recent assurances.

Keats: Assurances.

Haydon: Oh yes.

Keats: From a patron?

Haydon: Not just a patron. The Patron.

Keats: Who?

Haydon points upward.

Haydon: Divine assurances!

Keats: Ah.

Haydon: Last night in my painting room Raphael appeared to me.

Keats: The Angel Raphael.

Haydon: No! Raphael! Raphael! The greatest painter in history! My presiding spirit! And from 'neath his velvet cloak he gathered a globe of swirling mist, and bade me meditate upon it, until, just beyond my vision, what do you think I could see?

Keats: Uh, the divine face of Christ?

Haydon: The grandest conception of Christ's visage ever seen! Until *Christ's Triumphant Entry into Jerusalem* is complete, I will have but one patron! God! And I promise you, once it is exhibited and sold, I will see to it that you will not want for a thing for as long as you live.

Keats: I could never repay you for everything you've taught me about art, Haydon. But since we've touched the subject, I hate to ask, but the money I lent you—my brother is unwell as you know, and the winter has been very long, and any small amount you could manage—

Haydon: Let's not talk about who owes who what, it's in a poor taste. No, when I have made myself immortal through great works and the time comes to depart this life, I shall be your presiding spirit. For now, Shakespeare will have to do for you.

Keats: Shakespeare.

Haydon: Who else would preside over you? Shakespeare!

Keats: I've been reading Homer . . .

Haydon: Ridiculous!

Keats flips through his notebook.

Keats: I wrote a sonnet. Here. Much have I traveled in the realms of gold, and many goodly shapes and kingdoms—

Haydon: Where did you get it? Who gave you the Homer to read?

Pause.

Keats: Hunt.

Haydon: Hunt! I should have known. It's no good. You can't just read whatever you're given willy-nilly. At this stage you're like wet plaster, everything sticks.

Keats: I asked to borrow it.

Haydon: You may borrow my copy.

Keats: You pawned your copy.

Haydon: I won't have some dilettante molding you to his whim. Next thing, he'll be forcefeeding you Miss Austen's latest twaddle.

Keats: Did you read it? It's quite good.

Haydon: I know. Damn her! And damn the Prince Regent's patronage of . . . ladies novels! This is what he calls high art—that is the problem with this country. No vision! Art should inspire even the lowliest citizen to elevate himself! This will be our mission! Swear it.

Haydon hauls Keats up on a pedestal.

Haydon: Swear. In the sight of God and the treasures of the Parthenon, swear to apply yourself to the cause of your art with the fullness of your whole heart. Swear!

Keats: I'll do it.

Haydon: Swear! Swear!

Keats: I swear.

Haydon: For if you do not, the heavens will weep, and your genius will ever sit upon your chest like a nightmare. Swear upon the chisel of Phideas!

Keats: I swear upon the chisel of Phideas.

Haydon: You and I are Colossi, Titans of the Arts, we stand astride the river of High Destiny, with one foot planted in the classical perfection of Ancient Athens, and the other here—London, March first, 1817—the day the mighty course of history was changed forever!

Keats: By what?

Haydon: The publication of your book, of course!

> *Keats jumps down.*

Haydon: Your book will be the lightening-bolt to art this country needs! We stand on the brink of a new and glorious era for art. I declare a new pinnacle for civilization! London is the new Athens! We are the new Greeks! Say it with me! We are the new Greeks!

> *A guard approaches—Apollo in disguise.*

Keats: Uh, Haydon?

Haydon: Here, amongst these ancient guardians, these silent historians, the mists are stirring! The faint Olympians awake! Oh take that down too, that's good, we wouldn't want that to be lost.

Guard: Quiet, please gentlemen.

> *Keats jumps down but Haydon remains on the pedestal.*

Keats: Sorry!

Haydon imitates the guard behind his back.

Guard: Or I'll ask you to leave.

Keats: Sorry, sorry.

Guard: Other people are trying to enjoy the museum today.

Keats: We were just leaving.

Guard: So keep it down.

Keats: Yes, we will, sorry.

Guard: Down from there, sir.

Haydon: Have you any idea to whom you are speaking?

Guard: No, sir.

Haydon: Perhaps you've heard of the man who influenced the men of power to purchase Lord Elgin's marbles for the Museum? C'est moi!

The guard looks to Keats.

Keats: Benjamin Haydon. The painter?

Guard: What, the one who writes those letters to the papers? All in capital letters? About how parliament should be thanked for spending thirty-thousand pounds to buy these stones, while the people are starving for bread in the streets?

Keats: Yes, that one.

Guard: Are you his keeper then?

Keats: No, I'm his . . .

Haydon: Protégé!

Keats: Haydon, will you—

Guard: Don't matter if he was the Prince Regent, sir. He can't climb on them statues.

Keats: Come down. Or they'll throw us out.

Haydon: Never! I refuse to descend to his level!

Keats: Don't be ridiculous.

Haydon: Ridiculous! I'll tell you what's ridiculous! That this . . . peon! Yes! This peon gives me orders! Perhaps you haven't heard, sir, Men of Genius are put into this world to give orders, not to take them!

> *Keats reaches in his pocket and pulls out some coins. He gives one to the guard.*

Keats: I'm sorry for your trouble. We won't be much longer.

> *He gives the coin back to Keats.*

Guard: Keep it. You need it more than I.

Keats: Why do you say that?

Guard: I am the watcher of thy sleep and hours of life.

> *The Guard exits. Haydon gets down from the plinth.*

Haydon: Well, la! That was a bit of fun—did you see when I did this? Or when I did this—did you see that? Priceless! Oh, don't tell me you missed it. That would be a tragedy. Think up some ruse to bring him back, I'll do it again so you can see. Oh for heaven's sake, what's the matter with you today?

Keats: Nothing.

Haydon: Don't let this fellow's boohooing upset you. I've heard it all before. 'Ordinary people have no use for art! Boo Hoo! The common man goes hungry! We are lazy and mother-hen Britannia should shovel food in our greedy beaks as if we were baby sparrows in a nestbox! We protest! We'd rather fill our bellies with free bread and beer than have to look at art!'

Haydon sits next to Keats and pats his hand.

Haydon: Don't worry. I'm not offended. I know how ignorant people can be. That's why we are artists, hm? High is our calling, friend. Great is the glory, for the strife is hard.

Keats looks at the coin.

Haydon: Listen here, if you're going to be wet blanket upon these wonders, I'll be off to my painting room. Genius takes no pique-nique— *Christ's Triumphant Entry into Jerusalem* awaits! I said, *Christ's Triumpha*—Lookee here, what's that? An advance, perchance?

Keats: No. I quit.

Haydon: You quit?

Keats: I cancelled my exams, pawned my tools, my books. Everything. I've quit medicine. I'm not going back to school.

Haydon: You're really going to do it.

Keats: I was so sure this was what had to be done, but now that I've done it—I fear I've made a terrible mistake. Tom is so ill. I don't know how we'll live, Haydon.

Haydon: May God bless you, dear boy. May God bless you.

Haydon kneels to pray.

Haydon: Bless his endeavour, oh bountiful Lord. Guide him on his difficult journey. Bestow upon him but a fraction of those gifts you have entrusted to me in your mercy.

Athena enters, dressed in the fashionable Grecian style. She walks around the marbles.

Haydon: Let him know the divine joy that pierces the heart, that cheapens all mortal happiness. Allow him one second of the exquisite and supernatural state of communion I have felt with you in my painting room, when your hand has guided my brush and the colours seemed to stream through the handle and it was as if the top of my skull had lifted and fireworks shot from my brains into the heavens! And then, the indescribable . . . the most pure and beautiful truth, pouring in, liquid golden truth and beauty, a million exquisite drops of beauty, dripping like an elixir into my skull as if I were an amphora. Then have you shown me the true face of Christ, in a mist, just beyond my vision, but so close! I reach for my palette and it fades, it fades! When will you reveal it to me, oh Lord? When?

Athena approaches Keats.

Athena: What are you looking at?

Keats: Uh . . .

Athena: Silence.

She grabs the ends of his scarf.

Athena: What is this ghastly attribute?

Keats: A muffler?

Athena: What does it signify?

Keats: My sister likes to knit?

Athena tightens her grip on the scarf.

Keats: I have a sore throat.

Athena: A sore throat. You are dismissed.

She throws the end of the scarf in his face. Keats slinks away.

Athena: Pathetic beasts. They stink of their own filth.

Haydon: This I most humbly pray, Oh Lord. Amen, amen, amen.

Keats: Haydon, get up. I think we should go. I'll take you to sup at the Museum Tavern, my treat.

Haydon: Hm? Sup, did you say?

Keats: Yes.

Haydon: But must it be the Museum Tavern? It's so crowded now at every hour.

Keats: The Old Mitre, then.

Haydon: So stuffy.

Keats: Lamb & Flag?

Haydon: A bit far.

Keats: Pillars of Hercules?

Haydon: Crawling with dramatists.

Keats: Wherever you like, then.

Haydon: No, no. Your treat, you choose. Ah! Don't look now.

Keats: What? Who is it?

Haydon: The Siddons.

Keats: Sarah Siddons? The Actress? That explains it.

Haydon: You never saw her?

Keats: Never.

Haydon: I was at her most recent farewell performance. She put down the candle in the sleepwalking scene! Can you believe it? So she could—

> *Haydon wrings his hands with a pained expression.*

Haydon: Actors! They ruin Shakespeare's characters! How can they live up to the truth and perfection of the reader's imagination? I stormed out at the interval, and swore never to enter a theatre again.

Keats: But you go twice a week.

Haydon: It was an innovation! Inferior artists follow the base urge to innovate, when they need only go futher down the path already illuminated for them by the masters.

Keats: Mrs Siddons is a very famous artist.

Haydon: You call that art? On what evidence?

Keats: Surely acting is an art.

Haydon: Look around you! Art, real art, endures. Literature endures. Music, a tricky one, but it has an enduring "something" about it. Theatrical spectacles? Over in a blink.

> *Athena examines the broken statues, then strikes a pose of mourning.*

Haydon: Look at her. Youth gone, looks gone, striking her famous classical pose. That's attitude number six of eight, I believe.

Keats: Don't you feel she has a sublime, majestic air about her?

Haydon: Yes, like a great ruin.

Keats: Haydon!

Haydon: I call them as I see them. This is my gift and my curse.

> *Hephaestus enters, in regency dress, walking with a stick.*

Keats: She is a lady of great influence. If she's come to admire the marbles, the common man will follow. That's what you want, isn't it? To elevate the taste of the nation?

Haydon: Yes yes, but see who she's with!

> *Keats looks.*

Keats: Who?

Haydon: Byron.

    Keats looks again.

Keats: That doesn't look like Lord Byron.

Haydon: Who else do you know with a club foot?

Keats: But the beard . . .

Haydon: He's been abroad. Self-imposed exile. It's all the rage with the literary set.

Keats: They look . . . strange.

Haydon: They're *in cognito.* Celebrated persons do this all the time, so they can walk about in public without attracting throngs of admirers. That can be very troublesome, I've found. I'm thinking of having a set of false mustachios made, once my great picture is placed before the public eye. You should consider something along those lines, something discrete in the Van Dyke manner. Yes, that will suit you.

Keats: It comes in patchy.

Haydon: You don't grow it yourself, that's the point! You have one fashioned, by a professional, out of mouse-pelts.

    Hephaestus approaches Athena. She tries to shoo him away.

Athena: I told you not to follow me. Go home.

Hephaestus: I can't, you have the key.

Athena: I need time to think.

Hephaestus: You look beautiful, in your disguise.

Athena: Really? It makes me feel puffy. Who will they take us for, I wonder?

Hephaestus: If I were a man, I would take you for the Queen of the City of the World. Come away from this place, Bright Eyes, it makes you sad. Come with me, we'll walk in the streets. See the sights.

Athena: I am not a tourist, Hephaestus. I am on a mission of vengeance.

Hephaestus: Come walk with me. There are markets with walls of glass, globes of fire light the street. Beautiful things. Lenses to see the very small, or to see into the heavens.

He shows her a pocket watch.

Athena: What is it?

Hephaestus: Mechanical timepiece.

Athena: What use do you have for a timepiece?

Hephaestus: Take it apart, see how it works. I'll make one for you, all gold, to wear round your neck, engraved with an owl, in an olive tree. Inside, it will read "For the bride who ran from me". And you will be the minute hand, pressing forward, and I will be the slow hand of the hours, and I will pursue you slowly.

He takes her in his arms.

Hephaestus: Be mine.

Athena: I cannot.

Hephaestus: Why not?

Athena: I am The Maid.

Hephaestus: You don't always have to be The Maid.

Athena: Being the Maid is an all-or-nothing proposition. Besides, you are married to Aphrodite.

Hephaestus: Ditty hates my ugly face. Calls me clubfoot.

Athena: You asked father for Ditty, and he gave you Ditty.

Hephaestus: Her beauty made me blind, mad. I only ever wanted you, Bright Eyes. You said if I gave you the key—

Athena: We'll talk about that later. When the business is over.

Hephaestus: We could be happy.

Athena: We don't need to be happy, we're immortal.

Hephaestus: Men are happy.

Athena: That's because they can't see the future.

Hephaestus: Come on Bright Eyes. Zeus sleeps, he won't see. He sleeps.

Athena: "I will turn my back on the world, and sleep. And my children will watch over me until I wake, and never set foot in the world of men, nor show favour to a hero. Lost without our influence, they will destroy each other and the world." I tended father for a thousand years. And this is my reward? It must be a test. To see if I can temper my vengeance with the justice of heaven, as Father would. Why such a cruel test, for a daughter so faithful? I must not be too hasty. I will find the punishment that fits the crime—then Father will awake and restore my glory.

Hephaestus: Things fall to ruin, Bright Eyes. Time is unkind to the works of men.

Athena: Time? Men did this. Where were my heroes to defend me? When they raised their eyes to me I ran to their aid. I turn my back on them for a moment, and look at what they do. They've turned my temple inside out.

Hephaestus: Don't cry, Bright Eyes.

Athena: I'm not! It's this hideous atmosphere! It makes my eyes water.

Athena wipes her nose on her sleeve.

Haydon: I never knew for certain they were intimate, but this confirms my intuition. Now come. *(loudly)* Some people don't know how to behave in a museum. They spoil the enjoyment and enlightenment of others.

Keats: Don't! Let's go!

Haydon: But you must speak to him!

Keats: To Lord Byron? What would I say?

Haydon: That you are a great admirer and a fellow poet! That you adore *Childe Harold's Pilgrimage* and can't wait to read the next canto! That your first book is published today! And perhaps he would provide a few words of endorsement for the second edition!

Keats: I'm not going to ask him that.

Haydon: Why not? Genius must push itself forward, or forever be lost in the crowd. I myself am naturally a very shy and reticent man, but through great effort I have learned to overcome these tendencies when there arises an opportunity to make an impression! Here is your chance! Be bold! Introduce yourself. He'll know your name soon enough.

Keats: He's *in cognito*—we shouldn't recognize him, out of respect for his privacy! And to ask him to read my schoolgirl scribblings . . . he'd annihilate me! He'd call me a dirty little blackguard!

Haydon: Fine, I'll do it then.

Keats: No! No, please don't. I'll go. I'm going!

> *Keats approaches but loses his nerve.*

Athena: You again. See how they've let themselves go. What now?

> *She wipes her nose on her arm. Keats offers her a handkerchief.*

Athena: What is this offering? A rag? Have you nothing to say for yourself, ephebe?

Keats: Uh . . .

Athena: Silence! You are dismissed. Go, go.

> *Keats backs away.*

Haydon: Ephebe? Must be the new slang.

Keats: It means 'beardless boy'

Haydon points at his chin again.

Haydon: You see?

Athena: Enough! Who is responsible for this abomination? Who is responsible for this?

Haydon: That's my cue—time to make my entrance! Toddle along, and I'll get you a proper introduction to your future patron. But don't go far. I know, have a look round the ancient urns. You can compose a little ditty, *Ode on a Greek Pot* or somesuch.

Keats: Fine.

Haydon: It is I, Divine Melpomene! I am the man! O Blessed Muse of Tragedy! Welcome to my humble parlour. I am as ever, your servant.

He bows.

Haydon: What a delight to see an old friend again! These wonders of antiquity could receive no greater homage than the attentions of our nation's arbiter of taste.

Athena: We have met?

Haydon: Yes! Of course! Benjamin Haydon! History Painter!

Pause.

Haydon: You surely recall that upon seeing my very large painting of *Dentatus* at the Exhibition that you declared it "Completely successful"? I'm now working on a much larger work, *Christ's Triumphant Entry into Jerusalem*—perhaps you would like to visit my painting room?

Athena: You serve Apollo, is that it?

Haydon: I beg your pardon?

Hephaestus: The great lady asks if you are an artist, Mr Haydon.

Haydon: What a delightful turn of phrase, may I use it? I am in league with Apollo. Indeed, we are on the most intimate terms. Now, have we met, sir? You do look vaguely familiar, yet I just can't quite put my finger on it.

Athena: This is Mr...

Hephaestus: Smith.

Haydon: Mr "Smith?"

Hephaestus: Aye.

Athena: Mr Smith is my . . .

Hephaestus: Brother.

Haydon: Is that so?

Hephaestus: Husband.

Athena: That was a tiny misunderstanding.

Hephaestus: Midwife.

Athena: Associate.

Haydon: Ah, yes. I see! What a great pleasure to meet you, "Mr Smith." And what is your profession, "Mr Smith?"

Hephaestus: Smith.

Athena: Mr Smith manufactures my . . . accoutrements.

Haydon: Smith by name, smith by nature. Charming! A good, honest craftsman, then, eh? Do you labour in the famous lady's stables, Mr Smith? When horse wants shoe?

Hephaestus: Peg don't need shoes.

Haydon: Peg? Is that your lady's trusty steed? Delightful! Oh! Now see my young friend over there. Come along, now! Come along! Don't be shy! Now this lad's father worked in a stable! What a coincidence! Though he was killed in a tragic accident, thrown by his horse, dead in the gutter by the side of the road, very sad.

Haydon drags Keats over.

Haydon: The poor little boy nursed his ailing mother, who died of the consumption, leaving four sad orphans! And now his brother is showing the signs. Tsk.

Keats: Haydon, please.

Haydon: But the plucky young fellow pulled himself up by his own bootstraps, out of that dusthole of misery and death . . .

Keats: Please don't.

Haydon: . . . studied medicine and educated himself in the classics of art and literature, under my vigilant tutelage—and now he's about become a published poet!

Athena: And you are his patron, Mr Haydon.

Haydon: I will be, once my great picture has sold, however at present I must devote my resources to the completion of my great picture, and content myself to be his mentor. Here, Keats, why don't you give us a little something?

Keats: What!?

Haydon: You know . . . a little sonnet or something, from your book.

Keats: You're not serious.

Haydon: That one addressed to me: "Great Spirits now on Earth are Sojourning!"

Keats: But I haven't a copy . . .

Haydon: I know it by heart, would you like me to do it?

Keats: No!

Haydon: Then extemporize!

Athena: Will you keep us waiting?

Haydon: Something about the immutable grandeur of beauty, that sort of thing. Go on!

Keats flips through his notes.

Keats: Aaaaaa . . . thing . . . A thing of beauty is . . . a constant joy. Its loveliness . . . endures until . . . the end of . . . time?

Haydon: May I interject?

Keats: What now?

Haydon: "Constant joy" . . . Wouldn't it be better like this: "A thing of beauty is a joy for*ever*?" "Ever" gives you a grander selection of rhyme— where can you go with "joy?" Toy, boy, ploy?

Athena: Annoy?

Keats: You're right, that is better.
A thing of beauty is a joy for*ever*,
Its loveliness increases, it will *never*
Pass into . . .

Pause. Haydon applauds.

Haydon: A sound effort—very Grecian, don't you think? It's not his best, of course—his little book includes diverse sonnets addressed to me, there you will see the glimmerings of an exquisite taste and sensibility in the making. I brought him here today so he wouldn't dwell upon it too much, it's a difficult time for him, on the eve of the launch of his brave little ship of poems on the foam of perilous seas. Will the wind of acclaim fill his sails? Or will it sink like a stone before it leaves the dock? It's a most terrifying moment for him, don't you agree? And he could really use a bit of encouragement. Perhaps from a seasoned craftsman. Like yourself, Mr "Smith." I'm sure.

Athena: Sit with the poor little orphan, Mr Smith. Rest your leg. Rest quietly. Do you understand? Quietly.

Hephaestus: Aye. If you need me . . .

Athena: I will not hesitate to call.

Keats follows Hephaestus to a bench.

Haydon: If I could express one fraction of my admiration for you and your long, long, long career on the stage. My friend here is more of an

Edmund Kean man, the young people and their new styles, you understand, there's no accounting for the taste of the young. But you, as The Grecian Daughter—tragedy personified! How we thrilled to the divine excess of your anguish! And as Isabella with her Basil-Pot. Every gesture, every word. Only genius.

Athena: Enough. You say you are responsible for this?

Haydon: For the marbles being here? Yes, I must admit, I am responsible, inasmuch as one selfless servant of Apollo, radiant god of all arts, can be responsible for influencing the efforts of many on behalf of a great nation. AH! Ahhhhh . . .

Athena: What is it?

Haydon: You were still and then—you moved! It gives one such a shock of delight, as if a statue had come to life. Behold, the line you create here. Phideas himself could not have arranged your drapery with more grace. May I sketch you madam, to commemorate your visit? Will you do me the great honour? We shall summon Apollo, eh?

Athena: Yes, summon Apollo. We'll see what he has to say for himself.

> *A small sound of a chime. Hephaestus takes out his pocket watch, removes it from its case, makes an adjustment.*

Keats: Strange weather we've been having. Don't you think? Mister Smith?

Hephaestus: Aye.

Pause.

Keats: I'll be glad when spring arrives.

Hephaestus: Every beast is glad for spring.

Pause.

Keats: Have you known the Great Lady for long?

Hephaestus: Oh, aye, we go back ages. Was there at her birth.

Keats: Really?

Hephaestus: Raised my axe and cleft the aching head of Zeus, out she pops in full armour.

Pause. Keats stares at Hephaestus' beard.

Hephaestus: What is it?

Keats: Just admiring your um. Beard.

Hephaestus: Hm.

Keats: The style is very uh . . . classical. Is it new? That is to say, did you acquire it recently? Grow it, I mean? Because it's very realistic, it doesn't look . . . Not like these new things people go about in made of . . .

Hephaestus scratches his beard.

Keats: . . . Mouse pelts?

Hephaestus returns the watch to its case and winds back the time. An elaborate new chime is heard.

Haydon: I pity you poor thespians, it's true. How sad that an actor's performance in a play can be but a temporary triumph, compared to say—the timeless works that surround us. Or a *painting*? Because the theatrical "aht" itself, and it's "ahtists" are, at best, ephemeral, don't you agree? Your work is destined to fade with the memories of those elderly ladies and gentlemen who 'were there.' And when they are gone, well—who can say what becomes of your legacy? Today you stand before us, a living work of art, a being of a superior order, dropped from a higher sphere. But tomorrow? Pfft! If only one could freeze you in time, capture your essence for eternity. Now that would be the thing, wouldn't it. The very thing. Oh no, oh no, that won't do at all.

> *Haydon arranges the hem of her skirt. The guard, Apollo, enters and does his rounds of the room.*

Athena: What are you doing?

Haydon: My study of the marbles has so refined my eye that errors strike it instantly.

Athena: I forbid you to touch the hem of my raiment.

Haydon: Well, la! Let's just leave it in the Dutch manner, then, shall we? Let's hope the soiled and crumpled apron adds luster to the milk pail.

Keats: I loved *Childe Harold's Pilgrimage*, by the way.

> *Hephaestus scratches his beard.*

Apollo stops behind Haydon and looks at the sketch over his shoulder.

Haydon: Perhaps if you just lifted your chin? A tiny bit, to the left, to reduce some of the—no, no, you're absolutely right, you are perfection, for a woman of your age.

Athena: I beg your pardon?

Haydon: The beauty of a young woman is delightful in its way, but it's oh, how shall I put it? Like a mouthful of some delicious sweet junket, that too soon becomes cloying. Whereas the beauty of a mature woman is more—savory. She may not win the beauty prize, but she has a natural dignity, a severe grace, unpolluted by sensuality, masculine. That's a compliment, you understand. Would you do me the great favour of holding your arm like this? As if you were holding a—

Athena: What?

Haydon: Bunch of flowers? Or, say, a trident?

Athena: What?

Haydon: You know, a three-pronged spear.

Athena: I know what a trident is. To assume Poseidon's trident as my attribute would be an abomination.

Haydon: As you will, milady. I'll rough it in for now.

> *Keats walks around a statue. Hephaestus joins him.*

Keats: Haydon speaks of them all the time, but this is my first time seeing the statues. Have you seen them before, sir?

Hephaestus: Aye. In the place they were made, long before they came here.

Keats: In Athens? Really?

Hephaestus: City of the World, once, as yours is now.

Keats: They must have been beautiful. In their day.

Hephaestus: Aye. Garments painted red-blue-green, skin alive with golden wax.

Keats: Really? Painted? Are you sure? Wouldn't it look garish, all that colour? It just doesn't seem — Grecian. I can't imagine it. Still, seeing them like this, in this room . . .

Hephaestus: Gives all the pleasure of seeing a beautiful lady, grimed and dressed in rags, with one arm, no legs, and blinded eyes.

Keats: Do you know the figures, Mr Smith?

Hephaestus: There sits the Old Man, Zeus, and Hera, his bitch. Demeter here, mourns her daughter, gone underground. Bright Eyed Athena, Virgin Warrior. Divine Intelligence. All this to the glory of Pallas Athena. This is her festival. Even the gods honour her.

Keats: Who sits with her?

Hephaestus: Her slave, old clubfoot Hephaestus, god of the forge. He would make anything for her, do anything for her. She thinks he's a toothless, three-legged dog she can whistle for and pet and kick without being bitten. His true nature is a secret.

Hephaestus spits on the ground.

Keats: Women.

Hephaestus: They're a poison tide that swallows up your industry, your strength, your ambition, your art. Avoid 'em long as you're able.

Keats: What about Apollo? Where is he?

Hephaestus: Paulo? Kept safe in some other place. He is responsible.

Keats: Usually, when I look at things long enough and empty my mind—that is to say, when I am open —things open for me. These stones are so important to Haydon, I'm trying to see them as he does. But they resist me.

Athena wipes her eyes.

Haydon: But lo! My lady weeps! Overcome by Phideas' sublime representation of the Three Fates!

Athena: Fates! It's this damp cold!

Haydon: A too delicious climate is unfit for the struggles of the soul! Travel abroad, go to Italy, they say. Why? Did Phideas leave Greece? Britain has the Elgin Marbles, at last where they should be, out of the hands of the barbarians!

Athena grabs Haydon's pencil.

Athena: What did you call them?

Haydon: Barbarians?

Athena: These stones.

Haydon: The Elgin Marbles.

Athena: The Elgin Marbles? Surely you are mistaken, I think you mean the sacred statuary of The Parthenon.

Haydon: Yes, yes, Lord Elgin's Marbles.

Athena: Ripped from a temple by desecrators.

Haydon: Removed with permission!

Athena: Whose permission?

Haydon: Lord Elgin had papers—an official firmin!

Athena: Firmin?

Haydon: Official . . . papers! From their government. No man but a martyr was ever treated so severely as Lord Elgin for his patriotic act of preservation—and what is his crime?

Athena: Dismantling the greatest achievement of civilization?

Haydon: Succeeding where others have failed for centuries.

Athena: You mean to tell me that the Greeks welcomed the rape of The Temple of Virgin Athena?

Haydon: Well, by 'Greeks' you mean the Turks, or the other barbarian hoardes who pass for Greeks these days. The real Greeks no longer exist, they have no rightful claim. Here in Britain we have had the foresight to bring civilizations' greatest achievements together in one place! One needn't traipse about the globe to see a holy relic here or a mummy there or a shrunken head in Timbuktu—just visit the British Museum! Here they are for safekeeping, not to mention convenience, in the true temple of Western civilization!

> *Athena gathers a ball of energy and raises her hand to smite Haydon. Apollo, behind her, catches her wrist.*

Apollo: Allo, allo. What's all this then?

Athena: You. I knew this was your doing.

Apollo: I hardly recognized you Thene. You look so . . . puffy.

> *She snaps Haydon's pencil.*

Haydon: Never fear, milady, never fear, I have another. Now if you could just reach down a bit, like this. As if you were . . .

Apollo: Stroking a lion?

Haydon: Very good! Very good! Yes, that's just the effect we're looking for. You're holding a trident and stroking a lion. Where will we get a lion?

Apollo: Natural History, Africa, 17 B.

Haydon: Who's for a change of scene? What do you say, shall we explore the dark continent together?

Athena: Oh, cease, cease, for Hades sake!

> *Athena holds up her hand. Haydon stops, and takes off his glasses.*

Haydon: Oh. I'm so sorry. I suffer from a bit of eyestrain, over-devotion to the great cause of art. If you'll excuse me.

> *Haydon stumbles away, covering his eyes. Apollo picks up his sketchbook and leafs through.*

Apollo: Not bad, not bad. The draughtsmanship is first-rate, look at this, how he handles the line. Exquisite. Why must he paint? And on such a scale? Giant paintings—he has gifts, but he just doesn't listen—he just goes skipping down the path least suited to his talents.

Athena: How long have you been here?

Apollo: Nearly the span of one man's life.

Athena: Times are hard?

Apollo: Why do you ask?

Athena: You found it necessary to take employment.

Apollo: Oh, this? No. It's temporary. So I can keep an eye on him.

Athena: Keep an eye on whom?

Apollo: A hero.

Athena: What did you say?

Apollo: You heard me.

Athena: A hero. A hero, in this vile, corrupted place? A hero, from these—sad little self-obsessed creatures? Can they fight? Could they throw a spear? With their grubby little hands, and pencil-stubs and—mufflers?

Apollo: They're artists. This is what they're supposed to look like.

Athena: So your hero is an artist, is that right?

Apollo: That's right.

Athena: Desecrator. You sacked my temple to give the spoils to your hero, to get back at me. You still can't bear it that I won the war!

Apollo: What war?

Athena: The Trojan War!

Apollo: That's ancient history!

Athena: Desecrator!

Apollo: You're one to talk! Dragging the body of my man Hektor through the streets.

Athena: It wasn't me.

Apollo: Oh, right, blame your big bad hero, blame Achilles.

Athena: They have free will.

Apollo: And you didn't have anything to do with it. No divine influence of any kind. No midnight visits to his tent, no whispering in his ear? It was a disgrace. Father wept.

Athena: How would father feel about this? Picking up grimy little beggars, shivering in the cold. "I am your Patron, Apollo the fortune-teller. I'll give you great gifts if you serve me. Bend over and take it like a hero."

Apollo attacks her. She deflects his blows effortlessly without touching him. She continues to smite him out of the room and exits with him.

Keats: "Who are these coming to the sacrifice? To what green altar, oh mysterious priest, leads thou yon mooing cow in daisies strewn." Ugh. I dread the reviews of my book. 'The latest deluded young poet of the Cockney School, pity he thinks he can write—let's hope he hasn't quit his day job in the apothecary shop!' But that apprenticeship has ended. And this one, with Haydon—I know what people say about him, but he taught me so much, he convinced me to go on when going on was impossible. What do I do? I feel like a comet, picking up speed.

Hephaestus: Time comes to break free of an orbit and be flung into the universe. See with your own eyes, be your own master.

Keats: Do you believe in presiding spirits, Mr Smith? Invisible hands that guide us, that sort of thing. Haydon believes in them. He says God told him he would be the greatest painter in history, that spirits appear in his room, urging him on.

Hephaestus: No mortal deed is accomplished without influence.

Keats: Inspiration comes from outside forces, you think?

Hephaestus: A man's gifts are his own. But before he looks to his own desire, he must ask what the gods want of him, and yield to their wishes, or he will suffer. Atē.

Keats: Atē. What's that?

Hephaestus: Madness. When a man looks in the direction of his hopes alone, he turns his back on bad signs. He does not see disaster approach.

Keats: But how can he know what the gods want of him?

Hephaestus: He cannot.

Keats:

> I had this experience—like a waking-dream—in the surgery, not a place to be dreaming, I know.
> A man was on my table. Through the window I could see the coarse wool blanket of cloud across the sky.
> I would open his temporal artery—to let the blood, relieve the pressure on his blinded eye.
> His blindness was an asset, he couldn't see my knife,
> I press my thumb to his temple,
> find the pulse, the place beneath the skin, and sink the lancet in to trace the living vein.
> Suddenly, a shaft of light pierces the cloud, falls across my shoulder and my patient's face, and I hear the voice.
> Real as my own, but at once from without and within, as if inscribed with light on the tissues of my brain.
> And instantly his name is on my tongue.

He said:

> *The scene returns to the surgery, Apollo is*
> *there in a shaft of light.*

Keats & Apollo: I am the watcher of thy sleep and hours of life.

Apollo:

I have placed my golden lyre at thy side.
Pick it up, and find that you can play,
And the vast unwearied ear
of the whole universe
Will listen in pain and pleasure
to the tuneful wonder.
Is't not strange that thou shoulds't weep,
so gifted?
What sorrow cans't thou feel?
Explain thy griefs to me.

Keats:

Why should I tell thee what thou so well
seest?
Why should I strive to show what from thy
lips
Would come no mystery?

Apollo: Know thyself. Sing first and last of me.

Keats:

And with a hand of light he pushes back
The hair at my temple, and finds the pulse
The place beneath the skin, and once
touched,
The room dissolves, and I am on a
mountain
Looking down on clouds.

I am in that state, you know the one, in a
mist
I feel the burden of the mystery.
Then suddenly the mist is blown away,
And wonders are no wonders to me.

The surgery vanishes as the lights come up.

Keats:
Then voice, and light, are gone
The room envelops me once more,
And I am alone with my patient.
My mind had wandered—I hadn't stopped
the blood.
And yet, there is no blood,
Just a perfect row of stitches,
Atop a graceful scar.
I bind his head to hide the miracle,
Pack my things, I'm in the street,
I've left my coat. I can't go back.
It's done.

Pause.

Does that sort of thing ever happen to you?

Hephaestus: Paulo has shown you your nature.
Now you will serve him.

Keats: What? Apollo? Serve him? How? Why me?

Hephaestus: Not so strange that he would choose
a healer-poet, as his priest. These are his arts. Did
you raise your eyes to him?

Keats: To Apollo? No! Well, maybe, a little. It was
an accident.

Hephaestus: Be careful when you call on the gods.

Hephaestus gives Keats a key.

Hephaestus: Take this.

Keats: What is it?

Hephaestus: Key.

Keats: What does it open?

Hephaestus: Not to open, but to lock an open chamber.

Keats: What chamber?

Hephaestus:
> Light through the keyhole is enough.
> Too much brings blindness, madness,
> Death to men.
> Athena has the black aegis upon her breast
> And she will have revenge.
> There is a rumbling in the earth.
> Dogs bark and birds take flight.
> Stand back, the mighty door will open
> soon.

Hephaestus exits. Blackout.

Intermission

Act Two

Haydon stumbles in and gropes about the room, looking for his glasses. Keats, calling for him, enters.

Keats: Haydon—what's the matter?

Haydon: Oh, la. Look who it is. You've forgotten me now that you've been taken under the great man's wing.

Keats: What? You forced me to speak with him, and I've humiliated myself a thousand times over. Are you all right? Are your eyes bothering you again?

Haydon: I must have strained them, last night.

Keats: Were you working late?

Haydon: I told you, Raphael.

Keats: Ah, yes, Raphael. Sit, let me see.

Keats tilts back Haydon's head and examines his eyes.

Keats: You shouldn't work by candlelight, I've told you.

Haydon: Genius does not loll about in bed till noon. You wouldn't understand.

Keats: Look straight ahead. Tell me when you can't see my finger any more.

Haydon: There. There.

Keats covers one of Haydon's eyes.

Keats: How many fingers am I holding up?

Haydon: Two.

He covers the other eye.

Keats: And now?

Haydon: I haven't patience for these games of yours! Time is of the essence!

Keats: Just stay still a minute, will you? Haydon! Hold still! Do you even know how bad your eyesight is?

Haydon: I refuse to listen to your apothecarianisms!

Keats: You've got tunnel vision in one eye . . . .

Haydon: It's been like that since I was a child! I'm used to it!

Keats: And you're all but blind in the other.

Haydon: And if I were fully blind I would be the first blind painter! And my glory would be made even greater.

Keats: Haydon.

Haydon: How much money do you have? I know you have some. You see the thing is, I have arrived at *point non plus* with the creditors, and I find that I am, shall we say, impecunious. What have you got?

Keats: About four guineas.

Haydon: I need to borrow it.

Keats: It's all that my brother and I have to live on. I just left a paying profession, at your urging. "To climb the cliff of poesy!" Remember?

Haydon: But your book! It cannot help but be a success! Your day of glory is at hand! You could borrow against the –

Keats: I can't. I musn't.

Haydon: Trust me! I have prayed on it and have had solid assurances. Your book will shake the gods from the heavens! Only moments ago you were carrying on so about how you could never repay me for the attentions I've lavished on you— wantonly, it would seem!

Keats: I already loaned you thirty pounds. That was all I had and all I could call in, and now I'm in debt as a result.

Haydon: Which I fully intend to repay once my great picture is completed and sold! And frankly, I am hurt that you would be so unkind to bring it up.

Keats: Look, take this.

He gives Haydon the contents of his pockets.

Keats: There. Take everything. It's yours.

Haydon: I'll pay it back.

Keats: Don't bother.

Haydon: It's just a loan, a down-payment on the canvas.

Keats: What canvas? You aren't planning to start another painting, Haydon? Before *Christ's Entry* is finished? You can't. You mustn't. Another will ruin you.

Haydon: I am already ruined. The only way out is forward. Upward! Your new friend is a wealthy man. Go, ask him what he will contribute to a glorious enterprise.

Keats: Oh, Haydon.

> *Keats exits as Athena and Apollo re-enter. Athena controls Apollo with an unseen force.*

Apollo: Ow! Thenie!

Athena: Put them back at once!

Apollo: I'm guarding them. It's just a loan.

Athena: It's theft! They will never give them back.

Apollo: The Greeks will come and ask for them back. This place will pack them up and ship them home. These are civilized people, Athena.

Athena: Civilized people do this?

Apollo: Your precious temple was in ruins, ignored by you. Being used for target practice. I saved them. It wasn't easy—I had to use my influence. Enlisted the locals, encouraged a few bribes, forged some papers.

> *She smites him in the eye with a flick of her finger.*

Apollo: Stop smiting!

Athena: You are forbidden to walk among men while father sleeps, Apollo.

Apollo: We are all forbidden. And why is that? Because one of the immortal children of Zeus can't be trusted to keep her temper.

Athena: I have the key.

She shows him a key.

Apollo: That's father's key?

Athena: Yes.

Apollo: You stole it from the Old Man's cold clenched fist?

Athena: I tended Father, ALONE, for a thousand years. Where were you? The others? Nowhere to be seen! Only Hephaestus remained, he told me my stones had been stolen. He took the key, so I could put things right.

Apollo: You made Huff steal it for you? And what did you promise in return?

Athena: That's none of your business.

Apollo: You told him you'd be his bride if he got you the key. Shame on you.

Athena: It's impossible. I've told him a thousand times. He doesn't understand.

Apollo: Don't toy with him. He's not stupid and he's not a beast. He's a god, with passions!

Athena smites him again.

Apollo: While you were playing the dutiful daughter, didn't you wonder where the rest of us were?

Athena: Off—gallivanting!

Apollo: Where? We were prisoners, abandoned by Zeus to die of boredom. Cut off from the world of men, the world of heroes, until . . . ta da!

Apollo shows her his key.

Apollo: Huff forged copies for all of us. Didn't he tell you? Mumsie, Ditty, Demi, Po-Po, Missy, Ari, Yawni, Hermie—you, me — ? Wait, don't tell me!

Athena: Hestia.

Apollo: God! I always forget her. Hestia! What is she goddess of, anyway? Housework?

Athena: Huff's not a schemer, like you. He wouldn't. Would he?

Apollo: For the Divine Intelligence you can be so thick. He sent us on ahead so he could be alone with you.

Athena: But I am The Maid—

Apollo: We know, we know! You are The Maid, The Maid, you just love being The Maid, don't you!

Athena: He would never do such a thing.

Apollo: Come on, admit it. Weren't you bored without the world and its little troubles, without the clever little beasts and the amusing scrapes they get into. Mortal admirers to sing your praises? Weren't you bored, Thene? Didn't you miss your heroes? The smell of them, their fire?

Hephaestus and Keats enter.

Athena: Hephaestus! Come away from the ephebe. I demand you attend me at once.

Hephaestus: Aye.

Athena: Have you met the museum guard?

Apollo: We prefer "docent" actually.

Hephaestus: Paulo.

Athena: Apollo tells me you've been very busy at your forge, Hephaestus. Making keys.

Hephaestus: Aye. Good to be busy. Helps pass the time.

Athena: What is this obsession with time? There is no time for us, we don't need to keep busy, to keep time, to pass time. We're immortal. We are the immortal children of Zeus.

Apollo: Well, Huff isn't. Mumsie spawned him herself, isn't that right, Huff? Out of her . . . leg? Or something?

Athena: Shut up. Did you make copies of father's key to the world of men?

Hephaestus: Aye.

Athena: For all of us?

Hephaestus: Aye.

Athena: And Paulo put you up to this, yes?

Hephaestus: No.

Apollo: I told you.

Hephaestus: But he was first to go.

Athena: And why would he leave his ailing father's side, when we have been forbidden! We have been forbidden to walk among men! We have been forbidden to show favour to a hero! "Lost without our influence, they will destroy each other and the world!" That is the prophesy!

Apollo: No, no, no. You've got it all wrong. Without OUR influence. Not "our" influence—Father's. It's the royal "we". THEY will destroy each other—that's us, They, not the men . . . WE will destroy EACH OTHER. And also the world.

Athena: I've had enough of you and your literary analysis.

Apollo: It's the beginning of a new age, Thenie. I've seen the future. Artists, inventors, scientists—visionaries, not warriors —they will be the heroes now. Isn't that right, Huff?

Hephaestus: Aye.

Athena: Don't take sides with him! He lies to you, Huff. You're so gullible—you let him take advantage of you, with his hocus-pocus and his fortune-telling.

Apollo: I *can* see the future, Thene. You know that.

Athena: Oh, yes?

>	*Athena smites him.*

Athena: Did you see that coming?

>	*Haydon shows Keats his sketch.*

Keats: What is it?

Haydon: The monumental portrait of Britannia! To commemorate the purchase of the statues and announce the new era for art! With the Siddons as my model! Sheer brilliance! How could she resist such an honour? Our money troubles will be ended! I'll pay for a nurse for your brother, and build you a little cottage in the Lake District, next door to Wordsworth! A bit far, how about Hampstead? No, too close to Hunt. Well, some place away from the city noise so you can write and rusticate.

Keats: Now, when you say monumental . . .

Haydon: To the glory of England!

Keats: So it would be very large.

Haydon: To the exact scale of the chryselephantine statue of Athena that once graced the inner sanctum of the Parthenon.

Keats: So say, forty feet tall?

Haydon: Sixty, sixty-five. To give a bit of the pedestal and the swirling heavens above.

Keats: So this will be the largest painting in the world, I imagine.

Haydon: The grandest scale for the grandest subject!

Keats: Expensive?

Haydon: Monsterously so!

Keats: Where will you hang this painting, Haydon?

> *Pause.*

Haydon: Don't be small minded. This Great Work will be the katalysis that will tumble the old notions of art, and incite the creation of grand new public buildings! Academies! Museums! Institutions for the common man!

Keats: And where would you paint it? Your room is tiny. You can't even stand *Christ's Entry* up against the wall.

Haydon: I'll paint it here, in this room, flat on the floor. Under the divine guidance of Phideas!

Keats: What about the common man? How can they visit the marbles while you paint?

Haydon: How ignorant you can be. Look around you. You forget my influence with the men of power! They will hear me.

Keats: They wouldn't hear you when Parliament debated the purchase of the marbles.

Haydon: They wouldn't hear me . . . I wrote letters!

Keats: Attacking those "Men of Power" who might have helped you. Listen to me, Haydon. Haydon! We both know that you are dangerously in debt to your creditors, your friends! They'll put you in prison. You don't have money to eat, let alone finish your "Great Picture"—and at the rate you work it may never be done.

Haydon: Careful.

Keats: Why don't you just ask to paint her portrait? She would pay!

Haydon: I will never stoop to ask for work!

Keats: Hear me out. A portrait on a reasonable scale, to hang in the exhibition? Surely you haven't burned all of your bridges at the Royal Academy. Haydon?

Haydon: What, you suggest I apply for membership in the Worshipful Brotherhood of Furniture Painters?

Keats: It would be a sensation. She's a celebrated person—it would sell! You could pay your debts!

Haydon: The debt is owed to me! This country owes me! I have sacrificed myself to its future glory!

Keats: This whole idea is absurd. Why are you so stubborn—use some common sense! Can't you see? Why can you never yield?

Haydon: I spent eight years studying and sketching these stones by candlelight while they rotted away in a Hyde Park garden shed! I was the only one who understood them! Who saw through the grime and rubble to see their true nature! I was their one true friend! And they were mine. They were better friends to me than you ever were.

Keats: I'm just trying to help.

Haydon: Oh, la! Look at me, I'm so very young and clever, and falsely modest, will I be a doctor when I grow up, or a poet? How ever will I decide?

Keats: I'm sorry.

Haydon: "I'm sorry, I'm sorry!" Keep this up, won't you? You'll make me hate you as I have loved you. You see, this is the attitude! This nation is great in everything but art. This is our duty! Help me make them see. If you can't—I'm ruined, do you understand? I need two hundred pounds just to glaze, frame, and exhibit *Christ's Entry*, once it's finished, but how can I finish? The duns are always pounding at my door. My landlord, two years without rent. My library, clothes, silver, all gone to the creditors. God challenges me thus to teach me humility, that I might bring it to bear when painting the face of my Christ.

Haydon prays.

Keats: I'll get you home, you should rest.

Haydon: I am an instrument at the mercy of a higher power. I cannot rest. He will never allow it. I am his vessel. He lifts me up, he fills me with purpose.

Keats: I'll fetch us a carriage. Wait here.

Keats realizes that he has no money.

Keats: Haydon. I need some of that money.

Haydon: Money?

Keats: The money I gave you two minutes ago.

Haydon: You can repay me later.

Keats: But I just loaned it to you.

Haydon: Fine, fine. Here. I suppose now you'll want me to pay interest on touching it. How about forty percent, will that be enough, I wonder?

Keats exits.

Athena: So this is your hero. A one-eyed zealot, in love with his own genius. You know, he reminds me of someone. Oh, that's right. Huffie's little friends. The little Cyclopes brothers, what were their names? Thunder-man, Bright-man, and the little shy one, with the lisp?

Hephaestus: Sooty.

Athena: What was that?

Hephaestus: Sooty.

Athena: Your help-mates in the forge, fashioning lightening bolts for father. They adored you, didn't they? But then someone killed your sweet little pets. Now, who was that?

Apollo: He killed my child.

Athena: Who? Little Thooty?

Apollo: Father killed my child. He threw the bolt that killed my child.

Athena: So you murdered the innocent, ugly little craftsmen. Huffie's only friends.

Apollo: I would have killed the old man. But he was strong then.

Athena: You would have killed Hephaestus.

Apollo: Never.

Athena: Immortality is so inconvenient when you feel like killing someone. Apollo says he's your friend, Huff. Should you trust him? He murdered your little pets while you were out. Shot his arrows through their eyes. That wasn't very nice.

Apollo: Don't, Athena.

Athena: Threaded their eyeballs on a pointy stick, and shot it into your front door. Now that was a nice surprise to come home to.

Apollo: Don't upset Huff.

Athena: You're a fine one to talk!

Apollo: What has he ever done to you? Nothing! Except make armour for your heroes and stroke your hair while you prattle on. He loves you.

Athena: That can't be helped. He knows that.

Apollo: Aphrodite is unfaithful to him.

Athena: Surely you jest?

Hephaestus: I am not a dumb beast.

Athena: What's that Huffie?

Hephaestus: I am not a dumb beast.

Athena: Of course you aren't, we never said you were. Did we?

Apollo: Look, I'm responsible for all this. I admit it. I used my influence and stole your ruins and brought them here. So smite me and get it over with!

Haydon: I beg your pardon, but if any man is responsible for the marbles being in this room, I am the man. It is through my influence—

Athena: Influence! Ha!

Keats returns.

Haydon: I'll have you know that one day, I will be remembered as the most influential painter of my generation. I have had assurances!

Athena: Assurances.

Haydon: "Fear not, I am with thee. Be not dismayed, I am thy God. I will strengthen thee, yea, I will help thee—

Athena: Do not seek to do battle with me.

Haydon: "Yea, I will uphold thee with the right hand of righteousness!"

Athena: Cease! Cease! I don't want to hear another word out of you.

> *Athena smites Haydon repeatedly but he comes back for more.*

Haydon: Fine. But consider the invitation to my painting-room null and void! Null and void!

Athena: Cease! Cease! Cease! Not another word!

> *Keats pulls Haydon aside.*

Athena: Apollo, in your vengeance for my victory in war you have taken that which was most dear to me. I would kill you, but you are immortal. So will I destroy that which is most dear to the destroyer. This is the justice of Zeus. Ephebe! Your friend, here. Is he a great painter?

Keats: Uh . . .

Athena: Answer me.

Keats: He is one of the great spirits of the age. I owe him so much.

Haydon: Dear friend.

Athena: Ugh. Can he paint?

Keats: He's taught me how to look at art, and literature, and nature—how to find truth in a line or a colour, or a word in a poem . . . how to discipline myself, how to speak my mind, how to focus on my goal. No matter what happens . . .

Haydon: What could happen?

Keats: He gave me the courage to try, and to fail, and to carry on trying and failing again and again, for as long as it takes.

Haydon: You are the only mortal being who understands me, who would never abandon me in my difficulties. The only man I could love with my whole heart.

Pause.

Athena: Can he paint, or can he not?

Haydon: Go on . . . speak. From your heart. That will be best.

Pause.

Keats: He's had so many difficulties.

Haydon: But I have overcome them! Isn't that right!

Keats: His eyesight—isn't good.

Haydon: Had a fever as a child, blind for six weeks, but I prayed for many hours each day, and a miracle occurred! God restored my vision!

Keats: Partially.

Haydon: I'm used to it! A minor inconvenience!

Keats: So sometimes he ignores certain principles of . . . proportion. And perspective.

Haydon: Don't you see, that's my style! Yes, yes, sometimes the legs may *appear* to be too small for the heads, but when painting an heroic figure, what's more important?

Pause.

Keats: I'm sorry, Haydon.

Haydon sits.

Athena: Painter, the well of hope from which you drink is nearly dry. You were given more than your mortal share of gifts, yet you insult us by choosing the one road least suited to your destination. Lift the mist from your eyes. Now you see as you should, into the secret chambers of your sorrow.

Haydon weeps.

Keats: What have you done to him?

Athena: Nothing. *You* have opened his eyes. Hephaestus, would you like to finish him off? An eye for an eye?

Hephaestus: That's not Apollo's man.

Athena: What's that?

Hephaestus: It's that one. Paulo's man.

Athena: Who, the ephebe?

Pause.

Apollo: It's my prophesy.

Athena: Your prophesy? What prophesy?

Apollo: That I will forfeit old and sacred thrones for the sake of loveliness new-born.

Athena: That thing? You must be joking.

Apollo: He's our priest! We'll live again.

Athena: Approach, ephebe.

Keats steps forward.

Athena: What is its name? Speak up!

Keats: John Keats.

Athena: Junkets? Junkets? What manner of name is this? A name for a pet dog.

Apollo: John Keats, Thenie. Keats.

Athena: I'll call him Junkets. The worthless piece of human scrap. You look like a beggar. What are you?

Keats I'm a . . .

Athena: Spit it out.

Apollo: He's a poet.

Athena: A poet. Worse than a beggar, one of the dreamer tribe. A poet as a hero.

Apollo: Yes.

Athena: What will he use in battle? Satire? Can you fight?

Keats: What?

Athena: Can you fight, can you fight, are you deaf?

Keats: Well, I could, I suppose, but I detest . . .

Athena: Oh, cease. At least the other one has a little fight in him. Come closer.

Hephaestus & Apollo: Don't.

Athena: Do as I say.

> *She grabs him by the throat, hauls him up, and smells his face.*

Athena: He has the smell of death about him, like a heap of rotting leaves. You are in the autumn of your life, ephebe. Or winter, is it, Paulo?

Apollo: Let him go.

Athena: Do you know who I am?

Keats: I thought I did—my friend said you were The Siddons, Mrs Siddons.

Athena: You friend is mistaken.

Keats: He sees poorly.

Athena: He sees wrongly. Perhaps I should reveal myself to you, hm?

> *A mist begins to rise around Athena. She is revealed in armour.*

Athena: I am the inner lamp, Pallas Athena. Right hand of Zeus, protector of Athens, Goddess of Wisdom and War. I will be avenged upon Apollo for his desecration of my temple.

Apollo: Apollo, lord of the Sun, poet-guardian, who on this lonely isle has been the watcher of your sleep and hours of life.

Athena: Apollo, who looted my temple of its treasures, to throw to his mangy pet dog, Junkets. As some kind of educational toy.

Keats: So he's not Lord Byron?

Athena: He is Hephaestus, God of Industry.

Keats: Thank god.

Athena: Silence! Apollo's paid you a few little visits, has he? That's nice. But he can't give you what you really want, like I can. He can't make you immortal.

Keats: Immortal?

Athena: You could be my consort—what do you say?

Hephaestus: But—you are The Maid.

Athena: Shut up.

Apollo: It's your nature, Thenie.

Hephaestus: He's right, my love.

Athena: Don't call me that!

Hephaestus: But I love you, my love.

Athena: I'm sick and tired of being The Maid. Just because I don't want some stupid, ugly, brutish, deformed . . . you!

Hephaestus: You said you'd be mine if I gave you the key. You promised.

Athena: I said that's enough. Immortality, yes or no.

Apollo: Don't listen to her.

Athena: That's what poets want, isn't it? To be immortal?

Apollo: But through your life's work? In praise of me?

Keats: So I'd . . . die?

Athena: Immortality is not for the living.

Keats: But I've hardly started . . .

Apollo: He doesn't have long as it is.

Keats: What?

Apollo: Man's time on earth is short, that's all I'm saying.

Keats: How short?

Apollo: Very. Your little lives are over in a blink. Death and the fates have dealt your years, we have no influence with them.

Keats: But what will happen to Haydon?

Hephaestus: Paulo knows the future. Ask him.

Keats: Apollo, what will become of Haydon?

Athena: Get on with it.

Apollo: I'll need a body. For the oracle. It's better that way, sharper, crisper.

Hephaestus: Higher definition.

Apollo: That's right.

Athena: Use that one.

> *Apollo sits next to Haydon and grabs him by the neck. They are bathed in light.*

Apollo & Haydon: Full thirty times shall Phoebus' cart go round . . .

Athena: Oh, spare us the theatrics.

Haydon:

> And on a summer night,
> Storm-filled, fury of Zeus,
> Sick with worry, debt and want,
> Haydon bids goodnight to wife and child
> Closes his study door
> And stands at his easel,
> Armed not with brush, but gun.

Keats: Haydon, No.

Haydon: And puts a bullet in his skull.

Keats: No.

> *Pause. Haydon's head falls slowly forward.*

Apollo: Oh wait, there's more.

Keats: More? How can there be more? He doesn't die?

> *Haydon's head snaps back up.*

Haydon:

> A moment later,
> Rising from the floor with bleeding skull,
> He staggers 'bout the room with desperate moan,
> Then finds a razor hidden in his desk
> And gasping slashes at his bloody throat
> Until at last he falls, unwept and
> Unrememberèd.

Keats: Unremembered?

> *Haydon is released.*

Keats: He struggles on another thirty years and no one remembers him? What about his Great Picture?

Pause.

Apollo: What great picture?

Keats: *Christ's Triumphant Entry into Jerusalem?* Does he finish it? Does he paint in the face of Christ at last?

Apollo: Finally, on his seventh try.

Keats: And how does it . . . turn out?

Apollo: Overworked—Christ has a pained—no, constipated face. The elbow of the soldier is quite good, and *your* portrait in the crowd is full of life. The donkey Christ is riding is superb. Really, the ass is the saviour of the piece.

Keats: Where will it hang?

Apollo: Cincinnati.

Keats: Italy?

Apollo: America.

Keats: A great museum?

Apollo: A school corridor.

Keats: A corridor?

Apollo: It's a sixteen by nineteen foot failure. Where else does one hang a bad painting that size?

Keats: Poor Haydon. What did he do to deserve such a fate?

Athena: Hubris. The crime most hated in heaven.

Keats: Can't you forgive him? Apollo? As a favour to me?

Apollo: We are not forgiving gods.

Keats: But you aren't his gods, the god he prays to. You're the Gods of Greece.

Apollo: We are the Gods.

Keats: But I am as proud as he! He doesn't even know! I know I have abilities greater than other men—I will be among the English poets, I'll do it. I'm not afraid of failure. I would sooner die than not be among the greatest. Isn't that hubris?

Apollo: In your case, no.

Keats: Really? No, wait. I can't bear it that he'll carry on so long with so much hope and faith and so little success—can't he be remembered for something? Or leave behind one great work?

Apollo: He has already.

Keats: A great painting?

Apollo: No.

Keats: The marbles? What—you mean me?

Apollo: He'll be a footnote, in your biography.

Keats: A footnote, is that all? For all he's done? It doesn't seem fair—I get a biography?

Apollo: *That* doesn't sound fair? Then I've got some bad news for you.

Apollo puts his hand on Haydon's neck.

Keats: Stop. Wait. Don't. Can I just ask questions, and you answer yes or no?

Apollo: I hate doing it myself.

Keats: Please. For me.

Apollo: For you, but only you.

Keats: My brother's health.

Apollo: Looks bad.

Keats: I knew that. I knew that. Next question: will I—love?

Apollo: Yes. And it will give you such pain and torment as can only be relieved by death.

Keats: That's good, I guess. That's something. Will I spend much time abroad?

Apollo: Yes. A lot.

Keats: Where?

Apollo: Rome.

Keats: Should I learn Italian?

Apollo: That won't be necessary.

Keats: How about my book?

Apollo: Book?

Keats: Will it be well-received? No—

Apollo: The reviews are just in . . .

Keats: Don't tell me.

Apollo: Whatever you say.

Keats: Fine, fine! Tell me! No! Don't! All right, go ahead!

Apollo: You sure?

Keats: Yes. Go on. Go. Go go go.

Apollo: The critics say: "We find it amusing to see what a hash the youngest poet of the Cockney School makes of the ancient mythology. If he had an ear for rhyme, a knowledge of grammar, and sufficient intellect to distinguish sense from non-sense, he might perhaps do very well."

Pause.

Keats: Anything else?

Apollo: Byron calls you a dirty little blackguard.

Keats: I don't care. It doesn't matter. It's my first book. "He might perhaps do very well." That's good, isn't it? It's encouraging. He's saying: if I attend to my faults and work hard to improve, one day I will become an established poet. Right?

Pause.

Keats: Just tell me I have time, to make myself remembered. Ten years is all I ask. I can do it in ten.

Pause.

Keats: What.

Pause.

Keats: What?

Pause.

Keats: Less than ten? Can you tell me without being specific?

Apollo: Enough time to make yourself remembered.

Keats: A little more specific. In years.

Apollo: A little more than three, and less than five.

Keats: Oh. I see.

Apollo: The seed has already been planted in your breast, it begins to take root.

Keats: Consumption. Is that all? Couldn't I—drown in a storm, or die fighting for a great cause? Something a little more—romantic?

Apollo: Those are taken.

Athena: Apollo says you're short of time, ephebe. I have a little gift that's mine to give. Do you dream of being awake, beloved-of-Apollo? I am The Awakener. The Divine Intelligence. All the mysteries and beauties of the universe, unlocked. Wouldn't you like that?

Keats: What do you mean?

Apollo: Leave him alone, Thenie.

Athena: I'm not forcing him to do anything he doesn't want to do, am I? He has free will—don't you? Don't you?

Keats: I—think so?

Athena: I'm waiting. What do you choose? A handful of years groping about in a fog—or one moment in the clear light of heaven.

Keats: What will happen to me?

Apollo: I don't know. You might survive. You might be torn apart.

Athena: Let's try it and see.

Keats: Yes.

Athena: Let him hear you say it.

Keats: Yes.

> *She descends on him with a vampiric kiss. He struggles as if he is being torn apart by energy, then goes limp as if barely alive. Apollo and Hephaestus stand up on his own, he totters. He touches his bitten lip.*

Keats: Ow.

> *The light changes.*

Keats: I can see . . . everything.

> *Keats reaches out then falls, barely conscious, into Apollo's arms.*

Keats: Apollo. How long will it last? All this?

Apollo: Not long, I think.

> *Apollo strokes Keats's temple with his thumb.*

Keats:

> Knowledge enormous makes a God of me.
> Majesties, agonies, creations and destroyings
> All at once pour into the wide hollows
> of my brain, and deify me,
> as if some bright elixir I had drunk,
> And so become immortal.

> *He dies.*

Apollo: Nice work, Athena. You killed the only mortal who could make us live again. Are you happy now? How will father feel about this? To take a man's life before his fated hour is a crime against Zeus. He will make you pay!

Athena: It's your fault! You . . . you . . . ruined my temple! You brought it to this horrible place! You're responsible! You should never have come.

Apollo: I was called, Thenie. We've been dead to men for thousands of years . . .

Athena: Dead to men? They are dead to us!

Apollo: Zeus didn't turn his back upon the world. The world turned its back on him.

Athena: It's not true.

Apollo: Then a mortal raised his eyes and called on me. And I went to him.

Athena: Paid him little visits in his garrett, no doubt!

Apollo:
    I told him to go on. That's all. Go on.
    I found him in a garden with his friends.
    They placed my laurel wreath upon his
    head.
    Some ladies came, he would not take it off.
    But wrote them sonnets, 'neath a gentle
    bower
    Of whispering trees, and raised
    A cup of claret to the mem'ry of the bards.
    At twilight, when at last he was alone
    He saw his image in a pane of glass,
    Snatched from his brow my sacred wreath,

And hung it on the spindle of his chair.
And there he closed his eyes and begged me,
Golden-bright Apollo,
Not to punish him for insolence,
But let him live, to praise me.
Though I had watched him since he was a child,
T'was then I loved, and pledged to comfort him.
To lead him gently to his fated path
So he could pour a balm upon the world.
Alas! His little story ends too soon,
And we can only mourn for might-have-been.
Poor poet-healer, torn from the bright sky.
A songbird in the talons of a hawk.

Athena: Someone take it away. Hephaestus. Throw it in the river. These empty shells make me sick to my stomach.

Hephaestus: Do it yourself.

Athena: I beg your pardon?

Hephaestus: I'll serve no child of Zeus.

Athena: But it's me. Your Bright Eyes.

Hephaestus: No more.

Athena: But Huffie.

Hephaestus: I'm finished now with you. You broke the laws and snuffed out Junkets' life. You toy with me, you treat me as your slave. You're worse than Aphrodite.

Athena: We'll talk about this later, Hephaestus, at home. When the business is finished here.

Hephaestus: The business is finished, and you have no home. Nor Paulo. Nor the others.

Athena: But you made us all keys.

Hephastus: The copies I forged for the children of Zeus are weak, for one use only.

Athena: What do you mean? One use?

Hephaestus: Useless now, used once. The door is closed for good.

Athena: We're trapped here? On Earth? Among men?

Hephaestus: Aye.

Athena: Are we still immortal?

Hephaestus: Aye.

Athena: So for eternity. Here. In this place.

Hephaestus: Aye.

Athena: Where's Father's key?

Hephaestus: Safe-kept, where it keeps the keeper safe.

Athena: Father! Wake! Father! Help! Your Bright-Eyed daughter begs your aid!

Hephaestus:
> He will never wake.
> For I am not a child of Zeus.
> Like Thenie I was born of one alone.
> And now I curse that day when you were born,

when I released you from the old man's
skull,
full grown to torture me,
while I was cursed to love.
My gifts wasted while the world
Turns slowly on!
Time passes, here the clever beasts invent
things on their own.
Where is the God of industry?
Reduced to making earrings,
Pins, and spoons!
The second time I raised my axe to strike
the head of Zeus, no girl popped out.
But ichor, blood of Gods, turned to dust by
too-long sleep.

Athena: You killed almighty Zeus? AI AI AI AI AI

Hephaestus:

After every child of Zeus had flown,
though ordered not to leave his side.
Last to leave, I took his pulse with my axe,
and so I take his throne.
And this is my revenge, children of Zeus.
You will live here, in the city of the world,
The world I will create.
And with my influence,
the iron stomachs of the factories
will roar with fire,
and the faces of men will be blackened with
coal,
and metal horses and birds will fill the
streets and skies,
and invisible currents will pass through

metal threads,
and all the things to be invented will be invented,
and the world of men will be the world I created,
and the heroes of this world will be my heroes.

Athena: But where will we go?

Hephaestus: Live on the street as beggars. You could have been the Queen of Heaven. Now keep away from me. I never want you in my sight again.

Athena: No, Huffie, please. I will be yours. I will. Like I promised.

Hephaestus: Too late. Two thousand years I've waited for you. Now I have work to do.

Athena: What about my statues?

Hephaestus: They will stand or fall, with or without you.

Athena:
Then I curse you. I curse you and your City of the World.
I curse this trifling age, this wretched nation and its gloom.
When these stones stood in glory above my city,
this nation had no name. Yet they insult me! Though I am a god!
And they will suffer! Suffer!
The black aegis is upon my breast,
and I will be avenged.

Everything you build, I will destroy.

Hephaestus: I will rebuild.

Athena:

I will go across the sea, find a hero,
Raise an army, take what is mine by force.
I will lay this city low.
Kill her sons in battle and rain fire from the
skies.

Hephaestus: I will rebuild.

Athena:

I will bring strife, confusion and cruel
death to spite your efforts!
London. City of the World.

She spits on the ground.

I will strip this city of its make-believe
glory,
Expose her for what she is, a thieving slut—
whose costume gown of tinsel masks her
rags and oozing sores.
Naked and hungry, begging for mercy, her
cries will be pitiful.
But Pallas Athena, protector of cities, will
smile and return to her weaving.
The heaving world will also turn away,
Sickened by the sight of her,
And curse the day it ever heard her name.
This is the justice of Pallas Athena, Bright
Eyed daughter of Zeus.
I pity you, pity you.

I pity every low beast that lies in the arms of this filthy whore.

> *She exits. Apollo gently arranges Keats' body and steps away.*

Apollo: Poor human nature.

Hephaestus: Come, Apollo. I have work for you. Walk with me through the rooms, show me the things that have been invented so far.

Apollo: Build your world alone, I'll have no part in it.

Hephaestus: Come now, Paulo.

Apollo: Your world is not fit for heroes.

> *Apollo exits. Hephaestus looks down on Keats' body, then kneels to pry open Keats' hand to find the key, which Hephaestus places in his own pocket. He gives Keats a shake.*

Hepheastus: Wake up.

> *Keats wakes up, but is very groggy.*

Keats: What?

Hephaestus: It's time to go.

Keats: All right.

Hephaestus: Back to the forge.

Keats: Back to the forge. Yes.

> *Hephaestus gives the waking Haydon his glasses.*

Hephaestus: Good as new. Better maybe.

Hephaestus exits. Keats writes furiously in his notebook. Haydon puts on his glasses and watches him write. Keats gives Haydon the notebook.

Haydon: For me? "To Haydon, On Seeing the Elgin Marbles for the First Time."

He reads silently.

Haydon: This is the most perfect expression of the artist's striving after the mysteries of the sublime that I have ever read—and you just . . . scribbled this out in a moment! Damn you! Damn your wretched genius! Such ease! You have only seen me in my worst habits of application—you have no idea of the fury of my early efforts. But I see it in you. You know, I play the mentor, John, but I am just—

Keats: Haydon, really . . .

Haydon: Humbled. So humbled.

Keats: As I am by your—

Haydon: No! No! Take my highest compliment! Do not throw it back in my face!

Keats: Thank you.

Haydon: You'll copy it out fair for me? That I might paste it in my diary? To commemorate this historic day? The day the publication of your book shakes the gods from the heavens?

Keats: Of course.

Haydon: I knew you would understand them as I do. I have so much more to tell you, now I know your level of appreciation. What say we pop into the next room and decipher the Rosetta Stone on our way out?

Keats: No more today. I'm starving. You must be hungry. Are you hungry?

Haydon: Now that you mention it, I could eat a horse. Shall we find one to eat? Your treat, did you say?

Keats: Museum Tavern. It shouldn't be too busy.

Haydon: It's always too busy, but we'll use our elbows, eh? Run on ahead, I like to bid farewell to my friends after a visit.

Keats: Go on.

Haydon: I won't be a moment.

Keats stands near the exit as Haydon prays.

Haydon:
Oh Merciful Lord, I thank you
For another day amidst the greatest glories
Of your creation. I humbly pray
to be the greatest painter of my country,
To fulfill the brilliant destiny
You have promised me.
And by the chisel of immortal Phideas,
I swear anew to devote the rigour of my life
To your glory, the glory of Brittania, and
The protection of these immortal treasures.
In this room I feel the ether of your
Supernatural power, it lifts me up;
Until I am hoisted up on the shoulders
Of the masters,

And placed atop the great wall of
posterity—
High above the hardened minds and
Petty difficulties.
From there, the vast idea before me
Is crystal clear, an endless vista
Unrolling towards a limitless horizon.
From this summit, cheered on by
All the Men of Genius who came before
me,
I will take up my chisel with a shout,
And with a mighty blow,
Crack the wall of history, through which
A small star of light might shine.
In awe and trembling,
I am ever your servant.
Amen.

> *Haydon touches the statues tenderly as he
> exits.*

Adieu, my friends. Adieu, adieu, adieu.

End

Program Notes

from Touchstone Theatre Production,
NOVEMBER 2008

To Haydon

On Seeing the Elgin Marbles for the First Time

by John Keats

My spirit is too weak — mortality
Weighs heavily on me like unwilling sleep,
And each imagin'd pinnacle and steep
Of godlike hardship tells me I must die
Like a sick eagle looking at the sky.
Yet 'tis a gentle luxury to weep
That I have not the cloudy winds to keep
Fresh for the opening of the morning's eye.
Such dim-conceived glories of the brain
Bring round the heart an undescribable feud;
So do these wonders a most dizzy pain
That mingles Grecian grandeur with the rude
Wasting of old time—with a billowy main—
A sun—a shadow of a magnitude.

The Parthenon Sculptures a.k.a. The Elgin Marbles

The Elgin Marbles have been at the centre of an international debate over the ownership of cultural property for more than 200 years. The Parthenon in Athens is one of the world's most recognizable landmarks, dating from the 5th century BC. It has suffered the ravages of time and war, and is now a protected historical and archaeological site. In the early 19th century, approximately half of the extant marble statues and decoration of the Parthenon were removed and brought to London under the direction of Lord Thomas Elgin, British ambassador to Constantinople. For several years the sculptures were displayed privately, but in 1816, Parliament agreed to pay £35,000 to purchase the marbles from Lord Elgin for the British Museum. In early 1817 they went on display to the public. Greece has repeatedly requested the return of the statues, but the British Museum maintains that they were obtained legally, are protected by law in the museum's collection, and are being held in their trust for the benefit of the entire world. A summary of the debate with links to both positions can be found at http://www.bbc.co.uk/history/ancient/greeks/parthenon_debate_01.shtml

Timeline
1815-1817

1815—The Battle of Waterloo, Napoleon surrenders to the English and is exiled to St Helena.

1816—"The Year Without Summer." Mount Tambora (in Indonesia) erupts, causing climate change, crop failure and death of livestock in the Northern Hemisphere.

1816—After lengthy debate, British Parliament votes in favour of the purchase of Lord Elgin's collection of sculpture from the Parthenon for the British Museum.

January 1817—The Elgin Marbles go on display to the public in a temporary gallery in the British Museum.

March 1817—During a sonnet-writing competition at Leigh Hunt's house in Hampstead, John Keats is given a crown of laurel leaves to wear. When he gets home, he writes a poem of apology to Apollo.

March 1, 1817—Keats' first book, *Poems*, is published. Haydon takes Keats to see the Elgin Marbles in the British Museum. Keats writes two sonnets after seeing them.

Character Bios

Benjamin Robert Haydon (b. Plymouth 1786—d. London 1846) decided to become a painter as a child, was largely self-taught, and became a well-known figure in the art world—as much for his outspokenness and criticism of the Royal Academy of Art (to which he was never nominated) as for his paintings themselves. It took him six years to complete what he presumed would be his masterpiece, *Christ's Entry into Jerusalem*, into which he painted portraits of many of his friends, including Keats and Wordsworth. In addition to his very vocal support of the Elgin Marbles, he championed state patronage for artists, the creation of a national gallery and public art schools, and recommended mandatory artistic education for politicians. Haydon is now recognized as one of history's great diarists.

John Keats (b. London 1795—d. Rome 1821) became a licensed apothecary in 1816, and studied surgery at Guy's Hospital. In 1817 he gave up his medical career to write poetry. The youngest of the great Romantic poets, Keats came from a working class background, and at an early age was attracted to classical literature and ancient mythology. While he wrote several epic poems, brilliant letters, and one unproduced play, he is best known for his shorter works, including "Ode to a Nightingale", "Ode on a Grecian Urn," "La Belle Dame Sans Merci," and "To Autumn," all written in one highly productive twelve-month period in 1818-1819. He had a famously tragic romance with his neighbour, Fanny Brawne, from whom he was separated when he voyaged to Italy for his health.

Pallas Athena (immortal) Of the Twelve Olympian Gods, Athena was considered second in power only to her father Zeus. Born full-grown and fully-armed from the head of Zeus, Athena was released from her father's head by a blow of Hephaestus's axe. Goddess of Wisdom and Righteous Warfare, Athena was known as the guardian of cities and civilization. The Parthenon, or Temple of Virgin Athena, on the Acropolis in Athens, was built (around 440 BC) to honor her and celebrate Athenian pride, under the direction of architect and sculptor Phideas. In her signature aegis, shield, and crested Corinthian Helmet, she was the inspiration behind England's personification of national pride, Britannia.

Hephaestus (immortal) is the God of the Forge, patron of craftsmen and industry, as well as the god of volcanoes (from his roman name, Vulcan). Born of Hera, his mother found him so ugly at birth that she threw him off Olympus, which crippled him. The only Olympian with a job, Hephaestus served the other Gods by making beautiful jewelry, thrones, robotic furniture, and armour for heroes. His help-mates in the forge were the Cyclops, a one-eyed race who made the lightening bolts of Zeus. Hephaestus was married to Aphrodite, goddess of beauty and sex, after Athena rejected him.

Phoebus Apollo (immortal) is the Olympian God of light, medicine, and art, and overseer of the nine muses. His golden lyre is often found on the spine of poetry books. Apollo was an expert archer had many unsuccessful love affairs with women, men, muses and other immortals. The most sacred site in ancient Greece was the Oracle at Delphi—where his priestesses delivered cryptic predictions of the future. Written on the wall at Delphi is the phrase "Know Thyself."

Sarah Siddons (1755-1831) was Britain's most celebrated actress, known for playing tragic heroines (and heroes—she was the first woman to play Hamlet.) Although one of the most famous women of the age, she managed her public image carefully and was considered the paragon of female grace, depth, and dignity. She retired from the stage in 1812, but continued to give private readings and performances, and as an artist's model she was the subject of many of the most celebrated portraits of all time. When she saw the Elgin Marbles, it is said that she wept.

George Gordon, Lord Byron (1788-1824) was the most glamorous and highly regarded of the "younger generation" of Romantic Poets (which included Shelley and Keats). His semi-autobiographical poetic travelogue *Childe Harold's Pilgrimage* (published in installments between 1812-1818) was a sensation, making him a household name. He was avidly against Lord Elgin's collection and the destruction of ancient sites by collectors and tourists. In 1816 he left England for good, and he died of a fever at the age of 36 while leading troops in the Greek War of Independence.

About the Playwright

Janet Munsil's plays include *Influence, Pride & Prejudice, The Ugly Duchess, Emphysema (a love story)* (UK title *Smoking with Lulu*), *Be Still, Circus Fire*, and *That Elusive Spark*. Her plays have have been produced in theatres across Canada and the UK, including Touchstone, Tarragon, ATP, Theatre Calgary, The National Arts Centre (Ottawa), the Univeristy of Victoria Phoenix Theatres, The West Yorkshire Playhouse in Leeds, and the Soho Theatre + Writers Centre, London. Her self-produced works, *Circus Fire* and *The Ugly Duchess*, have toured North America and overseas, most recently to Ireland and the Czech Republic.

Munsil is a graduate of the University of Victoria Phoenix Theatre program, where she studied directing and design. Since 1992, she has been the Artistic Director and Festival Producer of Intrepid Theatre in Victoria, BC, where she produces the annual Victoria Fringe Theatre Festival and Uno Fest: Canada's Singular Live Theatre Event.

www.ingramcontent.com/pod-product-compliance
Lightning Source LLC
LaVergne TN
LVHW041233080426
835508LV00011B/1182